KW-554-212

Border Collies

To red
(ignore this)

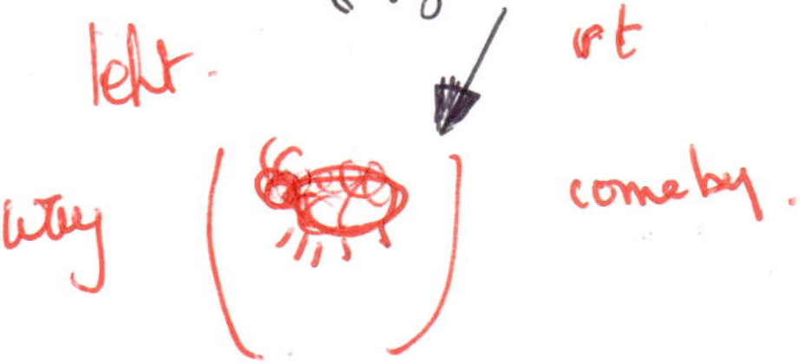

COME BY

Hamlyn **DOG BREED** Handbooks

Border Collies

Angela Sayer & Edward Bunting

HAMLYN

First published in 1988
by The Hamlyn Publishing Group Limited,
a Division of The Octopus Publishing Group plc,
Michelin House, 81 Fulham Road,
London SW3 6RB.

© Copyright The Hamlyn Publishing Group Limited 1988

All rights reserved. No part of this publication
may be reproduced, stored in a retrieval system,
or transmitted in any form or by any means,
electronic, mechanical, photocopying, recording
or otherwise without the permission of the
copyright holders.

ISBN 0 600 55795 2

Printed by Mandarin Offset in Hong Kong

Contents

Introduction

The Border Collie is a working breed and the majority of its members live on farms, many of them in the upland and mountain regions of Scotland, northern England, Wales and Ireland. Since the 1970s there has been a rapid increase in the number acquired as household pets and for showing, and the breed has had many successes in obedience classes for a good while longer than that.

Every Border Collie is the inheritor of many decades of selective breeding for the ability to control sheep or cattle, sometimes without the farmer even being there to supervise. The dogs seem to be born knowing what to do – to run wide of the animals, outflanking any stray individuals, and then to run behind and take up a position at the back, ready to drive the stock up towards the handler.

This work, with variations and refinements, gave rise to the tradition of sheepdog trials, in which nearly all dogs are pure Border Collies. These are full-time working dogs from farms.

Another job well performed by the Border Collie is mountain rescue work, in which the breed's tendency to 'cast out' wide of the path has enabled it to locate missing people in places where no other rescuer, human or canine, could find them. They have a tremendous scenting ability and desire to work, and can become quite obsessive about what they are doing, irrespective of hardships.

Border Collies have also been trained as guide dogs for the blind and perform this work excellently.

Dogs with an affinity for one type of work may not be suited to another. This has given rise to the concern that since people are now breeding Border Collies for purposes other than herding, the natural talent and toughness of the breed will be diminished.

Some dogs live only for their work . . .

It is certainly true that some first-class show champions are indifferent workers on the farm or hills; and there are first-class working dogs that would never win a show because of a 'fault' such as the wrong colour or conformation.

The Kennel Club has recognized the Border Collie as a show breed since 1976 and enthusiasts have voiced the fear that this will be the worst cause of 'softening' the breed and producing dogs that do not carry the precious ancestral skill in handling livestock. If this did happen, the working members of the breed would end up keeping all their talent, and the officially-recognized strains would become a separate population, in which dog-lovers sought excellence in a totally different way.

But this is not likely. Today there are many Border Collies at work on the farms who win prizes in trialling as well as the show ring.

. . . and others make perfect, playful pets

A good Border Collie looks alert, intelligent and athletic. Its movement is (as the standard says) 'free, smooth and tireless, with the minimum lift of feet, conveying the impression of the ability to move with great stealth and speed'.

The traditional colours are black and white, typically a white stripe down the face, a white collar and breast, white or black-and-white legs, and a black tail with a white tip.

There are dogs with tan patches (tricolours) and some with grey instead of black; blue and red merles (a merle has a 'marbled' look – the colour is splashed with small flecks of black); and there are a few all-black and all-black-and-white legs, and a black tail with a white tip.

If you keep a Border Collie as a pet or companion it will be a lively animal and will probably have more energy than you, so you may give as much exercise as you like. There is, however, no minimum: dogs are adaptable and provided you take an interest in your dog and understand the sort of instincts that drive it, it will live happily whether in a town, a village or in the country. Remember that the Border Collie, perhaps more so than most other breeds, has a keen desire for human company.

Breed standard

If you are interested in showing these fine-looking, hardy dogs, educate yourself first by going to a few open or championship shows to see how the winning dogs look. When the judge has reached a decision, you may still wonder what it is that makes him or her pick out one dog as the winner. The answer is the breed standard.

This is written and revised from time to time by the Kennel Club, in consultation with the breed clubs (see page 21), and describes the ideal specimen of the breed. However, no matter how carefully the standard is

There are two typical coat lengths

Border Collie

Ears Medium-sized and set well apart; semi-erect and mobile

Head Fairly broad in the skull; foreface makes up half the length of the head

Eyes Oval, set well apart; dark brown except in merles (i.e. flecked coat pattern) where some blue is permitted

Nose Black (black or brown in chocolate coloured dogs)

Mouth Strong, with a scissor bite

Height
♂ 53 cm (21 in)
♀ slightly less

Weight No standard for UK

Body Strong and muscular with wide, deep chest and broad back

Coat Moderately long-coated variety has a 'mane', 'breeches' and bushy tail; there is also a smooth-coated variety

Colours A wide range of colours, but all-white or mainly white dogs not accepted for showing

Hindquarters Broad and muscular; tail moderately long, curving gracefully down, with upwards swirl at end

drafted there may be misunderstandings in its interpretation. A judge has the task of deciding what the written word means in practice, and is therefore appointed on the basis of long experience with the breed.

We show here some of the main features of the breed standard in simplified form.

Some details from the breed standard

A good head

Correct slope of shoulder

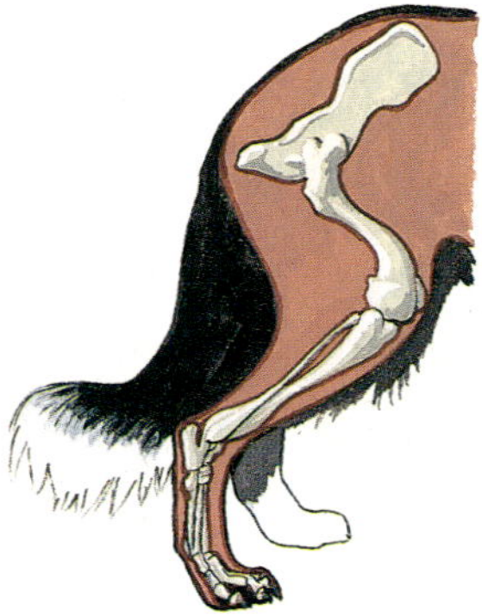

Correct angulation of hindleg

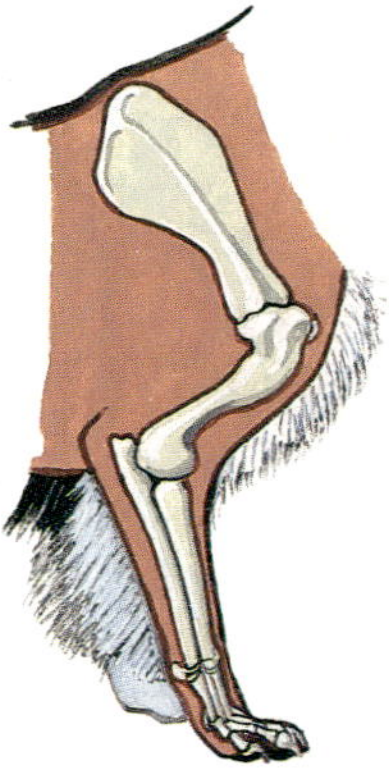

Registration, shows and trials

When a Border Collie puppy is born it is normally registered. If it is in a working strain it will be registered with the International Sheep Dog Society (ISDS) whose offices are in Bedford. The breeder fills in a form stating the pedigree, name and markings of the dog, and whether it is to be kept by the breeder or transferred and registered in another name. These details are entered into the ISDS Stud Book, which records the dog's colour, breeder, parents, coat type and date of birth.

A judge studies an entry at a show

If your Border Collie is to be shown in the ring, or if you buy a bitch to use for breeding future show dogs, you will need to register the puppy with the Kennel Club in London.

A working Border Collie is given a single name, and so for instance it might simply be known as 'Ted'. Those registered with the Kennel Club will have an affix to go with their individual names; the affix can be a prefix (before the individual name) or a suffix (after it). So the dog could, for instance, be named 'Plynlymon Ted' or 'Ted of Plynlymon'.

These names must not be changed and no two puppies in a litter may be given the same name; in the case of the Kennel Club names, the same one may not be used more than once in 10 years.

Types of show

Exemption show Dogs are exempt from the need to be registered with the Kennel Club – this is the only type of show where they are. It is the most informal kind of show, and is not held by a breed club, but a charity, an agricultural show, a village fete or the like.

Sanction show This is an informal, members-only show held by a local canine society or breed club. For example, the Camberley and District Canine Society held a sanction show on November 15th, 1987, at Maidenhead.

Limited show Also organized by a local society, but at a more formal level.

Open show Held by a canine society or breed club. When a canine society catering for a variety of breeds holds an open show, all these breeds be admitted. For example, the North-east of England Working Breeds Society held an open show in January 1988.

Championship show This is an open show, except that the standard is even higher and the proceedings are much more formal. The Kennel Club offers Challenge Certificates for the best of sex. If a dog wins three of

Scent discrimination test in an obedience class at Cruft's

these it is entitled to the prefix 'Champion' to its name. The Midland Collie Club's championship show was held in Stafford in February 1987. The Border Collie Club of Great Britain holds a championship show each year around March: in 1987 it was in Newark.

In addition there are the group and general championship shows: these are the really famous dog shows, with Cruft's at the top of the list. Other examples are the Manchester Dog Show or the Birmingham Dog Show. These shows are of less concern to the owner who is just beginning in showing.

Sheepdog trials

There are dozens of local trials all over the country, and the most successful dogs in these are entered in the national contests. Sheepdog trials began as part of the hill farming tradition: the conditions and work were modelled as closely as possible on those encountered in everyday sheep work in hill farming. However, today this does not necessarily exclude dogs that work in lowland sheep farming or cattle farming.

Even so, it has to be recognized that trialling is different from real-life shepherding. One difference is that trial dogs have to work small groups, typically of four or five sheep. So a dog that succeeds in trials is not necessarily (though it normally is) the dog that will work a flock of 100 sheep best. Shepherds or farmers often do feel that the winner was not the best dog, but they accept that in practical terms there is no other way to reach a decision.

Lifting sheep at a trial

Moving the flock ahead of the shepherd

The national trial is a 3-day event. It begins with a brace event in which pairs of dogs work the sheep over a set course; and after this it is all 'singles'. In the qualifying trials 5 sheep are liberated some 400 metres (yards) from the shepherd and his dog. The shepherd sends the dog to bring the sheep. The dog runs out on a wide detour known as the 'outrun' to outflank any stragglers and reduce the chance of them splitting away from the group.

After the outrun the dog comes round to a position behind the flock. He pauses, then brings them straight to the shepherd ('lifts' them). There then follows a sequence of manoeuvres: bringing the flock along behind the shepherd; moving it ahead of him taking the flock through pairs of hurdles; turning the flock; 'shedding' (with the shepherd's help, the dog separates two marked sheep from the five, all within a 40-yard shedding ring marked on the ground); penning the flock; returning the sheep from the pen to the shedding ring and shedding one marked sheep without the shepherd's help.

The 800-metre course at a national trial

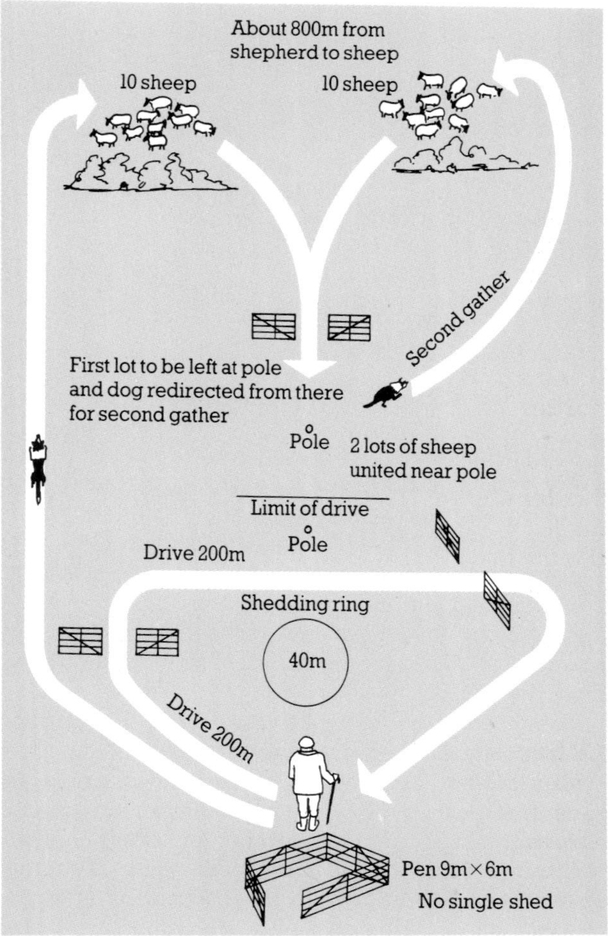

All this must be completed within 15 minutes.

On the third day, a Saturday, dogs that have qualified compete in a more difficult trial for a place in the national team. The course is increased to 800 metres (yards) and the number of sheep increased to 2 lots of 10. The dog must gather one lot first, bring it through a gate and then go back for the other; at a spot marked by a pole, the dog must unite the 20 sheep in one flock. The sequence of manoeuvres is similar to the one in the qualifying trial, but five sheep are shed in the ring, then penned and the single shed is omitted. Time allowed is 30 minutes.

The 15 highest-scoring dogs from England, Scotland and Wales, and 12 from Ireland (plus the Isle of Man), making a total of 57 dogs, then form teams in the international trials which culminate in the supreme championship. This event is held in England, Scotland and Wales in turn.

Breed clubs

Border Collie Club of Great Britain
Miss K E Lister, Fieldbank, 55 Waverley Road, Rugby, Warwickshire. Tel. 0788 72003

Border Collie Club of Ireland Miss J A Holmes, 46 Landsdowne Park, Templeogue, Dublin 16

North-west Border Collie Club Mrs J Richardson, Padiham Farm, Engine Lane, Shackley, Tilsley, Greater Manchester

Southern Border Collie Club Mr J Gascoine, 85 Faversham Road, Seasalter Cross, Whitstable, Kent

Other useful addresses

Collie Information Centre Oaks Corner, Common Lane, Hemingford Abbots, Cambridge PE18 9AP

International Sheep Dog Society (ISDS) A Philip Hendry and Co., 47 Bromham Road, Bedford MK40 2AA

The Kennel Club 1–5 Clarges Street, Piccadilly, London W1Y 8AB

A show-winning Border Collie is a beautiful example of this athletic breed

National Working Breeds Dog Society Mrs A Davis, 308 Hughenden Road, High Wycombe, Bucks
Royal Society for the Prevention of Cruelty to Animals (RSPCA) The Causeway, Horsham, West Sussex RH12 1HQ
Working Breeds Association of Wales Mrs G Mogford, Gwynfa, Pontymason Lane, Rogerstone, Newport, Gwent

Magazines

Border Collie Monthly B Swann, 284 Earlsdon Avenue North, Coventry CV5 6EX
Dog World 9 Tufton Street, Ashford, Kent TN23 1QN
Our Dogs 5 Oxford Road, Station Approach, Manchester M60 1SX
Working Sheepdog News The Editor, Ty'n-y-Caeau, Pwll Glas, Ruthin, Clwyd LL15 2LT

Choosing and buying

Where are good puppies sold? Make sure you start in the right place by obtaining addresses of reputable breeders through the breed clubs listed on page 21.

A good puppy should have, bright clear eyes, a damp nose and a silky coat in good condition

For most purposes, puppies are sold at around 8 weeks of age. Having found the whereabouts of a suitable young litter, make an appointment. Try to see them all, before the first ones have been taken.

Look at the condition of the whole litter, the mother and indeed the standard of cleanliness of the whole establishment. All the puppies should have bright, clear eyes, a damp nose and sharp, white teeth. The inside of the ears should be pink and shiny and the coat in good condition. Check the abdomen for a rash, and under the tail for signs of diarrhoea.

If the puppies are sleeping when you arrive, you will just have to wait until they wake up, for you cannot judge them without seeing that they are lively and playful.

Those buying a dog for working purposes are likely to look for a certain physical strength and go for the largest. For showing, be guided by the breed standard: the basic proportions of height to length, the shape of skull and the markings of the coat will not change from puppyhood to adulthood.

There is an instant bond that often arises between the visitor and one of the pups, and this can be a decisive factor in your choice. A dog instinctively responds to

8-week-old puppies for sale

Try to see the mother together with the pups

someone whose manner appeals to it, and that is the firmest foundation for a future partnership that you can get.

Taking good advice

The breeder and the vet are going to be your most important contacts with respect to the puppy, so listen to their advice. The breeder will give assistance in two areas. First, tell him or her whether you wish to select a dog with show potential, or just a good pet. If you are not looking for show potential, you may receive a puppy that suits you better and costs you less. On the other hand, the breeder will have a great deal to tell you if you are interested in showing.

Second, the breeder will want to be sure that his or her stock will be well looked after, and so is bound to give you good advice on general care.

As for the vet, it is best to call at the surgery early on and arrange for a home visit on the puppy's first or second day. If there is a choice, find the surgery that is convenient for transport in case of emergencies; but it is also important that your vet is the one you can talk to and in whom you can place your confidence.

Care of the new puppy

Choose a quiet day for bringing home the new puppy: visitors, birthday or Christmas celebrations and the like make it a confusing experience for a young puppy.

Food

The basic plan for feeding will be that as the puppy grows to its full size it will progress from having four or five meals a day to only one. One of the many advantages of buying from a breeder is that you can obtain a diet sheet stating what the breeder has given since weaning. It will probably also state the recommended diet for the first year or 18 months. See that you have stocked up with the first few days' supply of the necessary provisions.

There are many breeders all round the country who work by their own perfectly good methods of dieting and these may differ substantially from one place to another. Those who have bought a puppy from a pet shop would be best advised to get their diet sheet from the vet; but to print just one of the many possible ones here would be to give the false impression that all the others are 'wrong'.

Equipment

The puppy will need a bed, which in the first months is normally a cardboard box lined with newspaper – a large shoe box will do at first. The advantage of this is that as the puppy inevitably chews the box, you can replace it with a succession of larger boxes. Later, a basket will be more practical. Plastic ones are easy to clean, wicker or wooden ones make more work. Line the basket with a suitable blanket.

Basic equipment for the new puppy

Grooming equipment consists of a brush and comb, with the added refinement of a hound glove if you wish.

Drinking and feeding bowls need to be solid enough not to be overturned, and well made without cracks or seams where bacteria can lurk. Plastic or metal bowls, or sturdy earthenware ones, are suitable.

A play pen is very practical, for you can confine the puppy while you are busy with something else; you will need to place it on a layer of newspaper while the puppy is being housetrained.

The ultimate use for a shoe box

Other essentials are a collar and lead, and a bottle of household disinfectant for use on bowls and, where appropriate, uncarpeted floor surfaces.

The journey

Bring the puppy home by car if you can – that is, unless the distance is no more than a short walk, in which case you can carry it in a box or a holdall. Hygiene is the main reason – the puppy has not yet completed its vaccination programme and any contact with the ground is dangerous.

The puppy may be frightened of the car and bewildered by the experience of totally unknown sights, sounds and smells, while it has never before lost contact with its mother and siblings.

Inside the car, spread newspapers, as car sickness is common. Wrap the puppy in a blanket or place it inside a bag or box from which it can see outside. Slatted wooden fruit boxes are good for this.

Settling in

Morning is the best time to bring the puppy home, in daylight and before the puppy's first feed, which the breeder will probably hold back. This reduces the danger of sickness in the car, and improves the chance that the puppy will have an appetite with which to eat a first meal on arrival.

After a nourishing, warm meal, place the puppy where it can relieve itself without inconvenience to yourself. This is the first moment of its house training (page 33), so select the spot with this in mind. After this the puppy will probably be ready to sleep, so place it in its box.

The puppy has to learn to be by itself in a room, which is a totally new experience, and it may howl at first, especially during the first night. Go into the room and reassure it from time to time, but it is best if you can contrive to do this at times when the puppy is not howling. It is better if you can ignore the first night's crying, for that is probably the best way to ensure peace the next night.

Firm treatment is best if the puppy cries

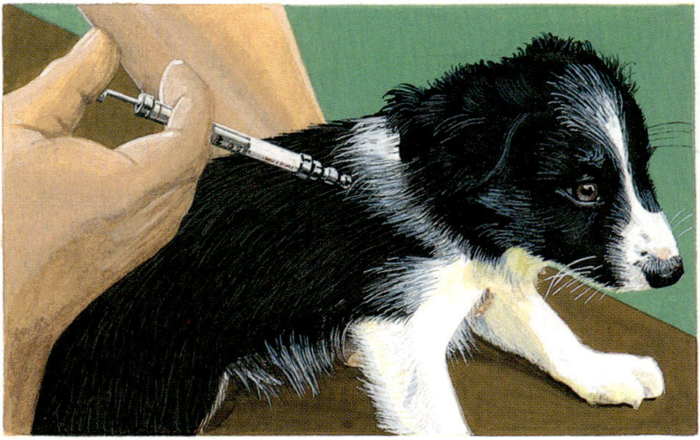

The vital protection all puppies need

Vaccination programme

The vet will be able to judge when the puppy is sufficiently strong to start its vaccination programme. There are six possible points in the programme: (**1**) Typically the first combined inoculation against canine distemper, canine hepatitis and canine parvovirus will be at 6–9 weeks, with a separate injection (first combined leptospirosis) on the same occasion.

(**2**) These two 'combined' injections will be repeated around 12 weeks. If the dog is likely to travel (or lives in) a country where rabies is prevalent, it will be given (**3**) a rabies vaccination at around 12 weeks. This is not normal for dogs living permanently in Britain or Ireland.

(**4**) A second rabies vaccination is given at roughly 14–16 weeks. The final routine vaccination during puppyhood, applicable only in certain cases as advised by the vet, is (**5**) a third vaccination against canine parvovirus.

The adult dog, having begun its life with the above protection, should receive (**6**) a combined booster vaccination against canine distemper, canine hepatitis, canine parvovirus and leptospirosis, around the anniversary of (**2**) above.

Puppies and children

Healthy puppies enjoy playing with children, provided they are kind. Teach the children how to groom the puppy; how to carry it correctly, with both arms encompassing the fore and hind legs; how to lift and put down the little dog; and how to help in preparing its regular meals.

There are a few basic rules to protect both parties:

- Children must be taught to wash their hands after play sessions with the puppy.
- The puppy needs a period of deep sleep after each play session, and children must be taught to respect this. Play periods will at first be about half an hour long. A puppy must never be allowed to become exhausted or overexcited.
- The puppy must not be allowed to play with items small enough for it to swallow or to get stuck in its throat.
- It must not be pulled around on a lead or treated like a toy.

Lead training should be fun for both parties

Training

A dog's obedience to a human owner stems from the long forgotten period in prehistory when the dog first came to link its own survival with mankind. Since then, obedience and work have been the dog's way to stay alive and protect its young, and it sees these things not as a form of servility but as its way of 'fending for itself'. So a dog will be happy if it is learning something, and all the more so if you ensure that the whole process is fun.

Kindness and encouragement are the key to successful training

Putting the puppy on its patch

House training

This can begin as soon as the puppy of 8–12 weeks has settled in its new home. The best method is to designate a special area, normally outside, as the dog's toilet area and try to see that the dog is placed there at all the predictable times when it will need to go.

These are:(**1**) first thing in the morning; (**2**) 5–10 minutes after waking from a daytime sleep; (**3**) about 5 minutes after each meal, but sooner when the puppy is only 8 weeks or under; (**4**) also put the puppy on its patch last thing at night.

Whenever the puppy performs in an acceptable manner, be sure to praise it warmly; but do not punish it when it makes a mistake; merely show that such behaviour is not pleasing.

Basic obedience training

The very best way to learn to train your dog is to enrol in a dog-training class. These cater for all standards from the basics to competitive obedience word and besides giving you thousands of ideas, they provide a chance for the dog to socialize too.

Preliminary classes cover the basic commands, walking at heel and coming to call, while those who wish to progress to showing may attend ringcraft lessons.

Basic training is essentially about teaching your puppy to be considerate and obedient, to come *immediately* when called and to have acceptable manners in the home. Play is an important aspect in teaching manners, and it is vital that your dog really loves and respects you, so that you become its 'pack leader'.

Serious training should begin when your puppy reaches 6–8 months. You will be able to graduate to ringcraft and formal obedience work whenever you wish.

Training for work

This can begin as early as 6 months, but 9 months is a more common age. Training for work with livestock is

Leaping a jump during obedience training

Good dogs show a natural interest in sheep

done in two stages. First the dog learns its own name and a few basic items of obedience: Sit or Lie down (working sheepdogs don't distinguish between the two), Come, Stay, No. After this it will be introduced to the sheep. It will learn to run out round them (the outrun) to the handler's right or left as commanded; to get up from lying down; to walk forwards, rather than running; to drop back; and to leave the flock alone.

As it grows to maturity the dog will lose any tendency it ever had to bark at the sheep (most decent pups don't anyway). This habit of working silently will remain with it for life. Instead of using its bark, the Border Collie will use the power of eye contact to exercise its control over the sheep. This talent is known as 'eye' and is a natural ability possessed by no other breed of sheepdog.

Another useful natural instinct of the Border Collie is to gather the sheep, which matches up with their own tendency to bunch together. Later on, when the dog has learnt every other move thoroughly, it will be taught the final skills – to separate a single sheep or a small group from the main flock ('shedding'); and to put sheep into small enclosures, pens or races.

General care

Feeding

Your routine for feeding will depend on the type, age, weight and number of dogs you keep, on how much and what type of exercise is given, and on the appetite of individual dogs. Your routine will evolve from the diet sheet of the first dog you buy (page 25).

A selection of foods

Trimming mats from behind the ears

There are good proprietary dog foods in the shops: (**1**) canned foods which must be supplemented with biscuit; and (**2**) dried foods or dog nuts which contain meat and cereals in a balanced diet. If you use dried foods you will need to give more water, as the dog fed on canned food obtains water when it eats. There are also less good proprietary foods on sale, so look closely at the ingredients list; on the whole, you will find that the more expensive ones are better nutritionally.

Alternatively, owners often cook meat for wholesale butchers. Bones are excellent value and come from the same source.

Do not give sugary foods to a dog as they are just as bad for its teeth as they are to your own.

At each meal, clear away leftovers from the previous one. Clean water should be available at all times.

Grooming

There are two basic types of coat, the smooth and the rough. The first will need to be brushed out every few days, but a bath is a rarity, only needed if the dog is truly

A bath is a rare event for most Border Collies

caked in mud or dirt. Rough-coated Border Collies need to be groomed more often, with both the brush and the comb – more like daily. Mats behind ears or in the leg featherings, and badly soiled areas at the rear end, can be trimmed off with scissors. Once again, bathing is still hardly ever necessary, as the weatherproof coat keeps in good condition of its own accord.

It may be helpful to bath puppies, though: use a mild shampoo, or a medicated bath care if you are worried about fleas.

Tartar on the teeth

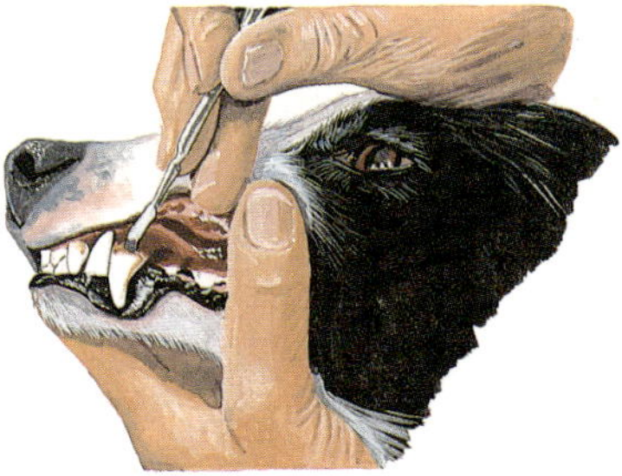

Teeth

The dog's teeth may be cleaned at regular intervals by rubbing with a slice of lemon or brushing with vinegar and water or salt water on a small toothbrush. A good diet with hard biscuit helps to prevent the formation of tartar on the teeth. If this does appear, however, have it scaled by the vet.

Fresh air, exercise and love – these are the essentials of general care

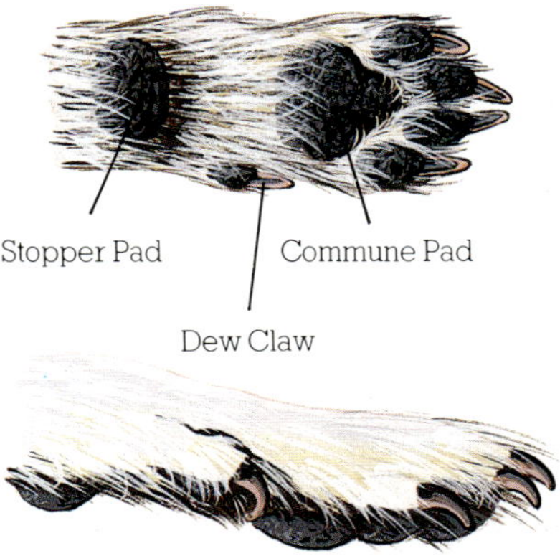

The dew claw is the dog's 'thumb' but serves no useful function

Ears

Examine these at regular intervals and clean out any dark wax, though you must never probe inside the ear canal. Look out for a greasy deposit, as this can be a sign of ear mites (page 57).

Dry swabs will usually lift out the dirt and wax, but you can use damp swabs for resistant grime, though water must never be allowed to trickle into the ear.

A dog that constantly shakes its head may have a grass awn or other foreign body stuck inside the ear and this might need the vet's attention.

Eyes

Minor eye infections are common: these cause soreness, a slight discharge and bloodshot eyes. Bathe with a saline solution that has been kept in a sterile container (make the solution by dissolving one level teaspoon of common salt in a pint of boiling water and allowing it to cool).

Treat each eye separately and do not wipe more than once with the same swab of cotton wool.

A more persistent eye infection will need antibiotic injections and an eye ointment, prescribed by the vet.

Nails and paws

Most Border Collies wear down their nails effectively with their bounding style of exercise, but those that spend much time indoors or on grass may grow their nails too long. The vet will be the best person to show you how to use the special guillotine-type nail clippers made for dogs' nails, avoiding the sensitive area of the nail (the 'quick').

Always examine the paws after exercise to see if the pads have been damaged or look sore. Small objects

Examining the paws after a run in the snow

such as a stone or piece of stick can get trapped between the toes, and it is best to look. In icy weather, remove any items that have lodged in between the pads along with ice and snow.

How to clip the claws

Breeding

Border Collies are generally of a very sturdy constitution and as long as you have picked a bitch who is healthy and fit, whelping should be straightforward. Make sure she has been tested and cleared of PRA and CEA, two hereditary diseases of the eye (page 59). See also that her hips have been checked for another hereditary disease, Hip Dysplasia (HD).

A bitch must be kept confined during her first season if unwanted litters are to be prevented

Finding the right sire is all-important

To breed good working dogs, owners search for the bitch and sire with the right combination of family connections, since good dogs usually come from lines that are known to possess excellent qualities. Those who breed Border Collies for show will also need these qualities, for the dogs must pass a test in handling sheep (albeit a simple one), or qualify in a national trial or be placed in an open one, before they may qualify as Full Champions. Those not gaining a sheep qualification may use only the title 'Show Champion'.

Oestrus and going to stud

The time at which the bitch becomes receptive to male dogs, and will mate and conceive, is known as oestrus or the oestrous cycle, and she is said to be in season or in heat. For most breeds the first oestrus occurs at an age of around 9 months but the Border Collie may not come into season until after 12 months, possibly even 18 months.

A good age for her to have her first litter is 18 months, and it is best for her to rest in her second season if she conceives a litter in her first. If she comes into season before she is a year old, it is best to see that she is not mated.

Make sure that the stud dog, too, is tested and certified free of PRA, CEA and HD. When you have found a suitable stud, keep in touch and let the owner know as soon as the bitch's season starts. One sign is that she becomes restless and affectionate; another is that her vulva swells or looks puffy, and soon it will have a red discharge (known as 'showing colour').

The oestrous cycle

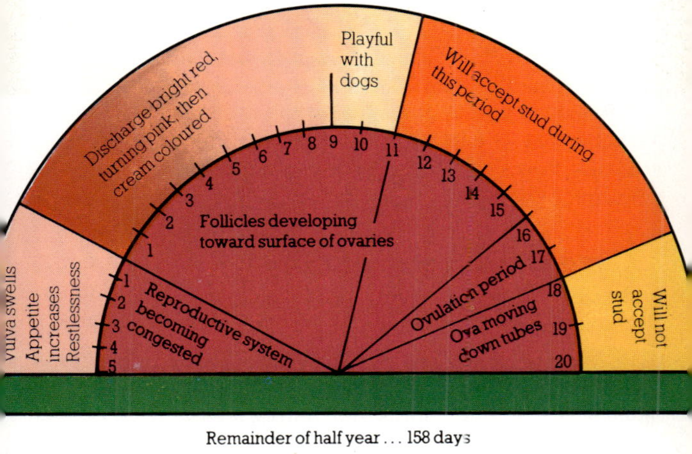

When this ceases and is replaced by a straw-coloured fluid, this is a sign that her fertile time has begun; but the most reliable sign is that when she is taken to the stud, she is willing to stand for mating.

The oestrous cycle lasts for an average of 21 days and the fertile period is normally from the 10th to the 14th day, though individuals vary a great deal. So book for the bitch to go to stud on the 11th day, and if possible book a second mating within the following 3 days.

Make sure the bitch is in the very best health and condition, and see that she is free of worms and external parasites. Give her nothing to eat within 3 or 4 hours of the mating, and see that she has the opportunity to relieve herself after the journey to the stud. Introduce the two, and from then on the proceedings should be under the charge of the stud owner, who may need you to help by holding the bitch.

Throughout the bitch's season it is very important to keep her under close supervision and to make sure that the planned mating is the only one that takes place. She is in constant danger of a casual mating with any male dog that may be loose in her vicinity. Such a mating is known as misalliance or mismating, and you have no way of knowing which one the bitch has conceived from, so it is usual to arrange for the vet to terminate the pregnancy and wait until the next season.

The average interval between seasons, for bitches of all breeds, is 6 months; but the average for the Border Collie taken on its own seems to be longer, perhaps 8 months.

Care during pregnancy

Border Collies are normally very lively and bitches usually retain their zest for activity for most of the pregnancy. Some, however, may go through a spell of being rather subdued and unwell, and it is common to have a loss of appetite, especially later in the pregnancy.

The puppies will be due after 9 weeks (63 days) but there can be variations of up to 12 days early or late.

If this is a first litter, the teats will probably give the first sign of pregnancy by swelling noticeably and becoming full of milk.

For the first 4 or 5 weeks there need not be any change in the diet of the bitch. Give her a mineral supplement from the fourth week. But although the diet and quantities are likely to stay the same, you should alter the distribution – give her two small meals, instead of one. Make sure she has clean, fresh water at all times, and take away food that is left by the time of the next meal.

Exercise should continue as normal, as long as the bitch is willing to go out, except that you should leave out the more vigorous activities involving jumping or 'sprinting'.

For the second half of the pregnancy you will need to increase the total quantity of food the bitch receives. Exact amounts may vary, but the food should be of the best quality. Make sure she satisfies her appetite, and you can add a third meal – a small snack at midday – if it is appreciated. However, should she appear to be taking up gluttony, you have to put a stop to this.

In the ninth week she will start looking for a place to have her litter, so provide a whelping box, lined with newspaper or loose straw. Place the box in a dry place and if the weather is cold, provide artificial heating. Central heating is usually adequate, but if this is not available hang a heating lamp over the whelping box.

Lighting should be dim but sufficient for the bitch to see the puppies, and the door should be kept shut to give her maximum privacy.

Delivery of the litter

As the onset of labour approaches the bitch may start to look anxious and she may instinctively tear up newspaper or even any fabrics she is able to get hold of, so keep her company and talk to her reassuringly. There is

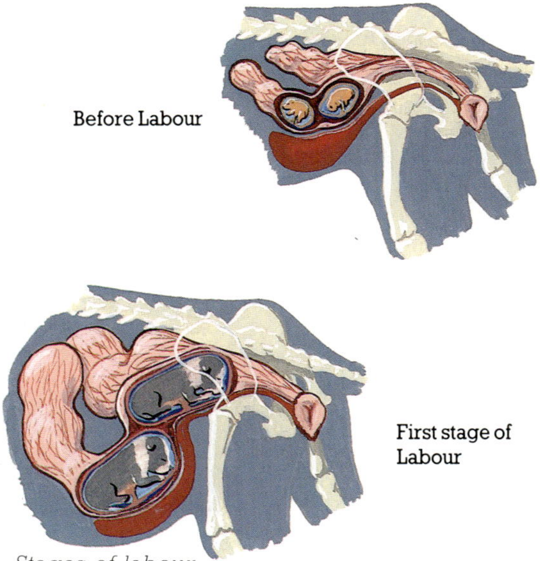

Stages of labour

a certain hardiness about the breed, and this is often evident in whelping, but for her first litter you may need to give moral support.

During the first stage of labour her cervix dilates and the puppies move down into position ready for delivery. The second stage is the actual delivery, beginning with her contractions in which she is said to be 'straining'. Note down the time when straining begins, as a reference in case anything should go wrong later on.

Normally straining lasts for less than an hour, and often it is as short as 5 or 10 minutes. The first puppy appears, enclosed in a membrane or 'bag' which the mother quickly licks away. In a perfectly normal case the only part you need play at this point is to praise the

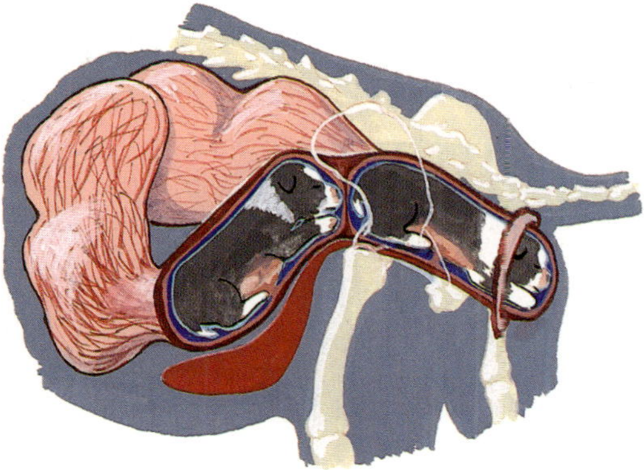

Normal Delivery

mother warmly and go and sit in the next room, out of the way. She will have ceased to need your company.

In normal cases the puppy, having had its mouth and nose licked free of fluids, cries and begins breathing in a matter of moments; then it squirms instinctively towards the mother's teats. A few minutes later the afterbirth follows, attached by its cord to the puppy. The mother will bite the cord off at the correct length.

The average litter is about 5, and the puppies are born either at regular intervals or in pairs or small groups, with a pause of ½-2 hours in between. Once all are born and suckling, bring a bowl of warm milk for the mother, praising her. Clear away and burn all the soiled bedding.

If things go wrong

Breeding is normally straightforward from start to finish, but there are occasional mishaps and it is impossible to predict when and to which bitch they will happen, so keep the vet's number next to the telephone, and give advance warning during office hours as soon as you feel labour is likely to start.

Puppies may appear lifeless, when all you need do is hold them upside to drain the fluid; or a young and inexperienced bitch may seem afraid of her first puppy and not want to suckle it, in which case put the puppy in a ready-prepared box with a hot water bottle, wrapped in a blanket. After a spell in the box, the puppy quite often becomes miraculously acceptable to the mother.

Keep a pair of scissors (sterilized) handy in case a distressed mother is tardy in biting off the cord. Other items on the table will be a bowl of warm water in which to wash your hands after touching the puppies; scales and a notebook in which to write down the time and weight of each birth.

The real emergencies are problem births, and if the bitch has contractions for more than an hour without any puppy appearing, you must send for the vet urgently. The vet may have to perform a Caesarian section to save the life of bitch and puppies. Similarly, if a puppy is part of the way out and the mother cannot complete expulsion, you have an emergency.

Worst of all, there is the rare possibility of losing the bitch. If she does die or is ill, or if she simply does not have enough milk for all her pups, you may save those puppies by quickly finding them a foster mother.

Hand rearing is an alternative to fostering but it is not an easy one, for it entails 2-hourly feeds round the clock and you will get little sleep for the first fortnight. However, if you take this course and get advice from the vet or anyone who has done it, and if you use the special foods and equipment that are made for the purpose, the puppies may come through against the odds.

Caring for the puppies

During the first 10 days, puppies have their eyes tightly closed and they do little but feed, eliminate and sleep. They will not be able to relieve themselves without stimulation from their mother, who does so by licking their belly and under the tail. At about 6 weeks they will learn to do without her help.

Suckling puppies in the whelping box

How to give a worming dose

Check the claws of the puppies at 3 or 4 days and again every 5–6 days, and if they look a little long they can be clipped, to prevent damage to the mother's teats as puppies scrabble for milk. Also check the navels daily for signs of inflammation or swelling. The dried cords will have dropped off after 2 or 3 days.

Once their eyes are open, the puppies begin to exhibit the first play behaviour, and they start to lift their bodies up on to their legs rather than squirming round in the whelping box. The first teeth come at 14–21 days and are needle-sharp.

At 20 days they can see and hear, and are well up on their feet. At this stage, socialization should begin and they will take a positive interest in their brothers and sisters.

Handle the pups gently and firmly, to get them used to you and to having all parts of their bodies examined: ears, teeth, coat, paws and underbelly. Give them their first dose of worming medicine at 3 weeks, and a second dose at 5 weeks.

To cater for the bitch's needs in lactation, feed her about double quantities in the first week, gradually increasing to at least treble in the fifth. She should be fed to appetite at least three times a day, and should have a good quality diet with added vitamins and minerals as advised by the vet.

The puppies should accept their first 'solid' food – baby cereal for example – at 3 weeks, and their demands on the bitch will lessen about the fifth week. At 4–5 weeks they will eat as many as four meals a day. Weaning should be complete by 6–7 weeks.

By 6 weeks they are walking firmly, playing and defecating without their mother's stimulation. The baby teeth are firmly established and they use them in mock fighting and to exercise their jaws on a chew or small bone such as a rib.

Their mother's enthusiasm will have gradually diminished from its initial maternal concern, and now she will want to spend only the briefest periods with her offspring. You should place them in a play pen, at first only for short periods, providing a few safe toys. Give water in good solid drinking bowls.

The weanling puppy

The period in a puppy's life between weaning and settling into its new home can be critical. It is a period of rapid development, both physical and mental.

Puppies are usually sold at about 8 weeks of age and it is important that fortnightly doses of worming medicine are given. These should have begun at 3 weeks and continued at 5, 7, 9, 11 and 13 weeks. Thereafter the puppy must be wormed at 6-month intervals.

The period of socialization is the period from weaning to about 14 weeks. It is during this time that the young dog learns to respond socially and to recognize its own species. Ideally, puppies should be taken from their mother and siblings at about 8–10 weeks, having enjoyed the first part of the period of socialization with dogs, while having the remainder in which to explore and develop lasting relationships with humans.

History of the Border Collie

The Border Collie is the most similar of the modern collies to the traditional ones that worked sheep up and down the British Isles for centuries. In the last 100 years or so this traditional collie has been split into five breeds: the Rough Collie, which is the tall, orange-brown one with the long fine nose and a very long coat; the Shetland Sheepdog which looks just like its miniature; the Smooth Collie; the Bearded Collie; and the Border.

Collies became famous when Queen Victoria kept them, her patronage doing even more for the breed than our present royal patronage has done for the Corgi. The Collie began to appear in dog shows around 1860, and the Queen had a show Collie called Gypsie.

The Border Collie's unique working feature is its ability to work silently, using eye contact with the livestock. This resembles the way gundogs 'point' game, for Border Collies stand motionless (although they shouldn't do this for more than a few seconds) and creep along as they eye the livestock, heads and tails lowered. This suggests that either Setters or Pointers, or possibly Spaniels, were used in the breeding of the first Border Collies.

The first recorded sheepdog trial was held in Bala in North Wales in 1873. It was an open competition and 10 dogs took part. The winner was a Scottish shepherd called Jamie Thompson, and his dog was named Tweed.

The most famous Border Collie of the last century was Old Hemp, born in 1893. Very few modern strains are not related to him and he sired well over 2,000 sons and uncounted daughters. His work with sheep was legendary. Another famous dog of that time was Old Hemp's son (and grandson) Tommy.

The International Sheep Dog Society was formed in 1906 by a group of shepherds and farmers from the Border counties of Scotland and England. They held the first international trial at Gullane Hill in East Lothian in that year, and except for the two world wars there has been an international every year since.

Trialling is concerned purely with the skill of dog and master in the field, and is a different world from showing. The only dog ever to have won three internationals (in 1934, 1936 and 1937) had one eye! This was Roy, whose master J.M. Wilson was the greatest sheepdog handler in all time.

J.M. Wilson, with his line of dogs, called the 'Whitehope' line, won 55 national and international trials

This 19th-century painting shows how the traditional collie used to look

Old Hemp

and 9 supreme championships between 1928 and 1955. His dogs became famous all over the world, and their names are seen on the pedigrees of many dogs today.

The Kennel Club recognized the Border Collie for showing in 1976 and the first member of the breed to qualify as a Show Champion did so in 1982. To gain the title of Full Champion, Border Collies must not only win three Challenge Certificates (thus becoming Show Champions) but they also must prove that they can work sheep fairly well. This they can do either by passing a special test specified by the Kennel Club or by qualifying at a national or international trial; thirdly, they may qualify by gaining a place in the top seven in an open sheepdog trial affiliated to the ISDS.

Today the breed is exported to countries all over the world: in Australia and New Zealand, they work alongside the local breeds of sheepdogs. They work the sheep on the Falkland Islands, and there are many Border Collies in South Africa, introduced there in the 1930s. Canada and the USA also have Border Collie populations and there are annual championship trials there. Other countries to which the dogs have been exported include the Netherlands, France, Switzerland, Germany and the Scandinavian countries.

Basic health care

Provided you keep a constant watch on hygiene and correct diet, and are continually aware of the need to avoid contact with poisons such as warfarin, metaldehyde, paraquat and any household supplies of solvents or acid, basic health care is reduced to manageable proportions. Preventive measures include regular checks and the routine worming doses and inoculations.

In cases of illness the vet will play a key role, for there are many cases when it will be plain for all to see that the dog is ill, but without the vet to diagnose the illness you simply do not know where to start. But here are a few of the commonest ailments, some of which you will be able to treat without outside help.

Ear disease Head shaking, scratching at the ears or the onset of an unpleasant smell may indicate a disease of the dog's ears. Healthy ears should be shiny inside with pale skin, free from dirt, wax or debris. Ear diseases must be treated without delay, to avoid excessive scratching, and to save the dog from the depression that may come with the constant pain.

Ear mites are described under *Mites*. Other diseases of the ear may be treated with antibiotic or anti-inflammatory drugs, plus an ointment or lotion.

Eye ailments Conjunctivitis is an inflammation of the lining of the eye; it is generally treated by bathing the eyes in a saline solution and applying antibiotic drops or ointment.

A foreign body may get lodged in the eye. One eye partially closed or watering may indicate the presence of a foreign body such as a grass seed. Once this has been identified you might be able to remove it with the corner of a paper tissue, or by flushing the eye with a syringe of warm saline solution. However, if there seems to be an object but you cannot see it, you will need the vet's help.

Blue-looking eyes (blue cornea) may simply be the after-effect of an infection, or of certain types of vaccination, but it might be caused by the formation of a cataract, which cannot be prevented and is difficult to cure.

Corneal ulcers can form and are so painful that the dog constantly rubs at the affected eye. The eye may be partially closed, with the third eyelid visible. Eye ointment can cure an ulcer, but persistent ones may require surgery.

External parasites

dog tick

follicular mite

louse

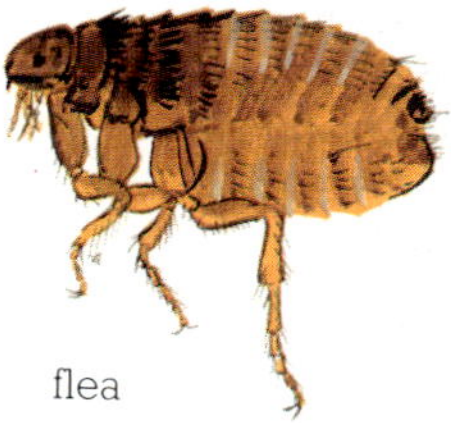

flea

Internal parasites, from l to r: (top) whipworm, roundworm; (bottom) tapeworm, hookworm. The whipworm and hookworm are not endemic in the British Isles.

Eye diseases (hereditary) (**1**) Progressive Retinal Atrophy (PRA) is the most well-known of these in the Border Collie. It only becomes evident at about 2 years of age (the age varies with the breed) and gradually worsens. Victims can go fully blind at 3 or 4 years, though some retain partial sight.

There are at least 2 different forms of PRA. The main one in Border Collies is Central PRA and the other form (Generalized PRA) is rare in the breed. PRA is sometimes called night blindness but this description is suitable only for the Generalized forms.

PRA has a recessive mode of inheritance – it is passed direct from parents to puppies, but can also miss some puppies, only to reappear in later generations.

All responsible breeders are attempting to breed PRA out of the Border Collie, and the main mechanism for ensuring this is the fact that the ISDS and Kennel Club will disqualify dogs from registration unless they have been recently tested and found free from the disease. For puppies, the fact that the parents have passed the test is accepted as grounds for registration, but as soon as any dog is found to have the disease its registration is cancelled.

(**2**) Collie Eye Anomaly (CEA) is increasingly found and it is a serious cause of blindness. Dogs affected with it can easily suffer a detached retina and go blind. A parent with a mild touch of CEA can produce puppies that are completely blind.

CEA has a recessive mode of inheritance and so it, too, is extremely hard to breed out; therefore the testing scheme applies to CEA as well as PRA. CEA can be detected at 9 weeks of age and can then disappear for life, so all pups should be tested at this age.

Fleas These small wingless insects suck the dog's blood and cause irritation and sometimes an allergic skin reaction. A heavy infestation has a debilitating effect on the dog due to loss of blood and lack of proper sleep; but worse still, any infestation at all can give the dog tapeworm, as the eggs of the parasite can be carried in the flea.

Special soaps, shampoos and sprays may be used to rid the dog of adult fleas in its coat, and the treatment should be extended to the dog's bedding and exercise areas to eradicate eggs and larvae.

Lice Another type of wingless insect that lives and breeds on the dog. Lice use specially adapted mouthparts to pierce the skin and suck the animal's blood and tissue fluids. You can eradicate the adult insects fairly easily with an insecticide, but they leave their eggs cemented tightly to the dog's hair and the only way to destroy these is to continue spraying with insecticide at weekly intervals until there are none left.

Mites More closely related to spiders than insects, these little nasties can cause intense irritation and depression. All species of mite are difficult to eradicate and you will in fact need to go to the vet for a prescription. Treatment must be kept up for a long time.

Sarcoptic mange is caused by mites that burrow into the skin, causing thickening and such intense irritation that the dog scratches and tears at the affected area, often breaking the skin.

Follicular mange mites attack the hair follicles, and in puppies patches of hair fall out around the head, eyes, muzzle and paws, while in older dogs the hair loss is more generalized.

Ear mites (*Odectes* mites) live in the ear canal. They can be particularly maddening for the dog.

Ringworm This is not a worm but a fungus that parasitizes the dog's skin. Dogs with ringworm generally have skin lesions (damaged places) that appear as roughly circular, scaly patches, where the hair has broken off leaving stubby ends. There may also be crusty scabs and pustules.

The vet will take a skin sample for laboratory analysis to confirm ringworm. Treatment is a combination of systemic drugs and skin dressings. Ringworm is contagious and transmissible to man.

Worms Even the best-bred dogs can suffer from internal parasites, which are known to us as worms. The first worming is against roundworm, which is commonly present in puppies. The medicine may be given at 3 weeks, then at 5, 7, 9, 11 and 13 weeks or even longer if necessary. Puppies affected with roundworms may have a pot-bellied appearance and suffer from bouts of diarrhoea. Fully grown dogs can be treated for roundworm at 6-monthly intervals, or a course of tablets can be administered as necessary.

Another, less common internal parasite is the tapeworm. One kind (*Dipylidium*) is carried by fleas, and another (*Taenia*) infects cattle, sheep and rabbits. A dog can be infected by swallowing an infected flea, or by eating the infected meat of cattle, sheep or rabbits.

The tapeworm's presence in the dog is generally discovered only when small segments of the worm, looking like live grains of rice, are seen around the dog's anus or in its bedding. The tapeworm is killed by dosing the dog with a specific medicine.

Index

Figures in italics refer to illustrations